SAYINGS OF
SATHYA SAI BABA

Edited by
David C. Jones

DETSELIG
ENTERPRISES LTD

Love is the seed, courage is the blossom,
and peace is the fruit that Sages grow
in the garden of their hearts.

Sathya Sai Baba

Sayings of Sathya Sai Baba

©2008 David C. Jones

Library and Archives Canada Cataloguing in Publication

Jones, David C., 1943-
    Sayings of Sathya Sai Baba / David C. Jones

Includes bibliographic references.
ISBN 978-1-55059-356-3

    1. Sathya Sai Baba, 1926- --Quotations. 2. Spiritual life--Hinduism--Quotations, maxims, etc. I. Sathya Sai Baba, 1926- II. Title

BL1175.S385 J66 2008   294.5'4   C2008-902555-5

Detselig Enterprises Ltd.
210, 1220 Kensington Road NW
Calgary, Alberta T2N 3P5

www.temerondetselig.com
Phone: (403) 283-0900
Fax: (403) 283-6947

We acknowledge the support of the Government of Canada through the Book Publishing Industry Development Program (BPIDP) for our publishing program.

We also acknowledge the support of the Alberta Foundation for the Arts for our publishing program.

COMMITTED TO THE DEVELOPMENT OF CULTURE AND THE ARTS

SAN 113-0234
ISBN 978-1-55059-356-3
Cover Design by Alvin Choong

Contents ଔ

Introduction –
The Idea of
Enlightenment

☙

"I do not know what I may appear to the world. But to myself, I seem to have been only like a boy playing on the seashore, diverting myself in now and then finding a smoother pebble or a prettier shell than ordinary, whilst the great ocean of truth lay all undiscovered before me." [1]

Isaac Newton, 1642–1727

"The idea of enlightenment is of utmost importance," said the sage, Nisargadatta Maharaj. "Just to know that there is such a possibility changes one's entire outlook. It acts like a burning match in a heap of sawdust. All great teachers did nothing else." [2] Light and Fire they taught – the Light of the illumined Self and the Fire that burns to ashes the false and limited self, a curriculum of Self-revelation and self-elimination, affirming what one is and deleting what one is not.

Sathya Sai Baba (b. 1926), the Indian spiritual master, told this story. "Lord Dakshinamurthy conveyed His message through silence. He seldom resorted to speech. By mere sight

He could impart the profoundest truths about the Universal and Divine. On one occasion in the course of travels, He reached the shore of the ocean. He was delighted to listen to the OMKARA vibrations coming from the ocean. The ocean represents the primal divine sound. It symbolizes the grandeur and majesty of the Divine.

"Dakshinamurthy drew a lesson from the endless waves reaching the shore from the ocean. He noticed that as soon as some rubbish fell on the ocean, it threw it out on the shore by a series of waves without retaining it even for a brief moment. Dakshinamurthy questioned the ocean: 'How selfish you are! You are boundless and fathomless. Can't you make some room for this poor stuff? It is highly selfish on your part not to tolerate this poor thing despite your vastness.'

"The ocean gave a fitting answer: 'Lord! There is nothing unknown to you. If today I allow this piece of dirt to remain with me ere long I will be filled with flotsam and jetsam and my entire form will be changed. Hence from the beginning I have to cast off anything that is dirty and polluting. Only then I can remain pure.'

"Likewise," said Baba, "every person should keep out even the smallest bad thought the moment it seeks the mind. To treat it as small and inconsiderable would mean allowing such things to enter the mind and in due course fill it entirely. In the process, the entire nature of the person is changed. His ... essence is undermined."[3]

Self-realization is the story of Dakshinamurthy's sea – that our essence might be expressed and the flotsam, expelled. No venture for the faint-hearted, intense perseverance, uncommon courage, and utter self-honesty are required. Are we willing to peer into ourselves to discover the discard? Are we willing to plunge into Lord Dakshinamurthy's sea and to be the purity of that sea?

Our real nature is Spirit, pure Spirit, and it cannot hold taint, toxin, or foreign matter, and still be itself. The foam and fragments, the sludge and the settlings of muck and refuse, all must be expelled – everything alien to that spiritual nature. The imperfections of our humanness – our doubts, our defensiveness, our self-diminishing thoughts, our resentments, regrets, foibles, fears, our judgments, condemnations, negativity, cynicism, our mistakes, misconceptions, misappreciations, our sense of lack and loss and unworthiness – all must be thrown upon the shore.

Evolving we are, from a neutral or loveless appreciation of ourselves, from a painful and punishing life, from tedium and pleasurelessness, from tension and strain, from a world of positivity and negativity to one of positivity alone. Evolving from a hundred wrong concepts about ourselves, from many things we think we cannot do and cannot be. Evolving into the inherent grandeur of our true Self, into pure Spirit, joy, love.

Even at age three or four, Sai Baba had a heart "that melted at human suffering." A beggar might appear, and

Sathya would rush from play and force his sisters to feed the poor soul. Sometimes his parents would shoo away a pleader before Sathya could help, but the boy would weep inconsolably until they recalled the starveling. Annoyed, his mother finally warned that if the beggar ate, Sathya would not, but the lad fed the outcast anyway. Said his biographer, "Nothing and nobody could persuade him to come to his plate, which was left untouched." [4]

Superhuman qualities of Sathya Sai Baba have been reported by countless witnesses in scores of books. Those who have spoken to him say he knows everything about them, hundreds attest to miraculous healings, and others say he has saved their lives, sometimes more than once. At will, he produces holy ash, or *vibhuti*, which has curative properties. Though he prefers Telegu, his native tongue, he seems to know every language, and has even corrected translators. He materializes gifts in the form of rings that fit perfectly (two I have seen) or bracelets, watches, fruits, or sweets. He is an incarnation of Love which he extends to everyone and everything.

One day some people drove Baba, then a young adult, to the jungle. A devotee recalled, "About four or five deer came near to our jeep, and I said that if I had a gun I would shoot them. Swami felt so bad about this that he did not eat for two days. From that day onwards we stopped shooting deer." [5]

Another time, a devotee brought a gift, originally procured for another, though deemed on second thought to be appropriate for Baba, but Baba refused it, saying, "No! no stolen articles, please."[6] To accept something intended for another amounted to theft.

Years ago a discouraged devotee told Baba, "The world is very cruel to me."

"That is its nature," answered Baba. "The purpose of the world is frustration; it has to engender need. When the need is strong enough, the individual seeks fulfillment."

"And fails!" cried the devotee.

"Only when he seeks fulfillment without! Within him, he can get it. The within is accessible always; it is ever responsible. There is pain only so long as attachment for outer forms remains."

Baba then spoke of something the devotee may not have understood – of how the mind had to neutralize its tendency to react "to something as pain and something else as pleasure" which then stuck in the memory and imposed a world of duality of grief and joy. It was the grief, the pain, that eventually drove one to Spirit, to the Power within.

"Which I can, at best, only hope to attain," the downcast devotee remarked.

"God asks for neither hope nor despair. They are subject to relativity. Universal Being is beyond both hope and despair, both certainty and doubt. It knows no lingering in its conclusions. It is ever flowing, in all directions, and in none of them."

Spirit did not career from positivity to negativity, from uplift to dejection. It simply was, and it did not know depression. It was free and flowing, expanding infinitely, never stuck on a single track, never stopped anywhere, never ended. Resisting this flow by clinging to old ways and concepts was a form of self-strangulation.

"What then shall be my direction?" asked the devotee.

"Take what works today for today. What works for tomorrow, tomorrow. One day at a time, each day for itself, each moment for itself, without a past, without memory, without conclusions."

"Conclusions?"

"Yes," said Baba. "Conclusions bind; they press on the mind. The newborn baby is not confined to conclusions. All conclusions enslave. Most men are slaves to the conclusions into which they have fallen."

Conclusions choked off further growth, further life, and they took many forms – concluding a single step as the final one, a single insight as the culminating one, a single judgment as the last word. But it was not just conclusions that were stifling the devotee; in fact, his mind had multiple conclusions, sometimes *contradictory* conclusions, as if it were divided against itself.

"Contradictions are inevitable," said Baba. "It is the very nature of this world and of the mind. But you can choose, either to be buffeted endlessly by the apparent contradictions or to remain in the calm centre of the cyclone. This is the problem of all problems, the problem of peripheral or central being."

"The circumference or the centre, the rim or the hub of the wheel?" asked the devotee.

"Yes, the hub is calm, steady, unmoved. But the mind will be drawn along the spokes, the objective desires, to revolve over mud and stone, sand and thorns. It will not believe that it can get bliss from the centre, rather than from the circumference, without undergoing a rough journey over turbulent terrain." [7]

In the centre was the Power, and once that fact was embraced, the turnings of the human mind could no longer wreak their havoc by alienating a soul from its own essence, or by whispering the ultimate heresy that the Spirit is weak.

Another day, Dr. John Hislop and Baba were driving to Anantapur, India, when they chanced upon a blind woman. Baba gave the woman some money, and the woman recognized him before he spoke, though two years had passed since his last visit.

"The woman seems to be happy," said Hislop.

"She was born blind but is always happy," answered Baba. "She has no worries."

"How could that be?" asked Hislop. "Look at her life. It must be a life of misery."

"Why?" said Baba. "She has no desires and is content. She does not know the life of a person who has eyes. She does not think that others are different from her. Her family is worried about her condition, but she has no worries."

"How could she not want a life different from that of a beggar?" Hislop persisted.

"Desires arise from the tendency of the mind to compare," said Baba. "It is chiefly the eyes, the vision, which presents to the mind opportunities for comparison. She is blind, her mind is not busy with comparison, so desires do not arise."

"If she continues happy and content," wondered Hislop, "will she be finished with [the reincarnating cycle of] life and death and be free at the time she dies?"

"No, that requires spirituality," responded Baba.[8]

It was one thing to be physically limited and to accept that with grace, and another to be deeply self-aware, meant Baba. The spirituality he spoke of would require the woman to understand that she was "the infinite potential, the inexhaustible possibility" as another sage put it. She would have to acknowledge her pricelessness, her limitlessness, her innate Power and Wisdom as Spirit. She would have to shed any misconceptions or misunderstandings inconsistent with her real nature, any diminished, damaged or flimsy notions of her self. Like Dakshinamurthy's ocean, she would have to divest herself of all that is false. Spirituality implies recognition of the true Self, and self-realization is simply acknowledging and living the life of that Self. The woman's contentment was a lovely beginning, but only with profound understanding of herself could she maintain that attitude in the face of the crises and challenges that might come in another life when she could see and compare. The self-realized are fully self-sufficient and self-assured – unassailable in any storm, undeterred in any circumstance.

Now the diminishment of desire is directly related to enlightenment because the self-realized person has everything already, so one who desires something with the thought that he is deprived or dispossessed does not know who he is.

It is the wanting of something, accompanied by the feeling of dispossession, deprivation, or undeservability that is at the heart of the problem of desire. Desires tend to focus one outward, not inward, to want what others have and to ignore what we have. In this sense, they misappreciate our own Self, and they underestimate the Power and Wisdom of our own Spirit. Guided by love, that Spirit may do whatever it wills, but an unawakened person with a flurry of desires is like a cornucopia stricken with envy.

Many are the avenues to enlightenment, but the key is to hold to one. "That student learns best and fastest who does not spend his time constantly shifting from one classroom to the next," concluded Baba, "You will learn everything worth knowing in my classroom."[9]

David C. Jones

1 Clifton Fadiman, ed., *The Little, Brown Book of Anecdotes* (Boston: Little Brown, 1985), 427.

2 Sudhakar S. Dikshit, ed., *I Am That: Talks with Sri Nisargadatta Maharaj* (Durham, NC: The Acorn Press, 1973), 100.

3 Tumuluru Krishna Murty, *Digest – Collection of Sri Sathya Sai Baba's Sayings* (Hyderabad, India: Dr. T. Gowri & Co., 1994), 186-187.

4 N. Kasturi, *Sathyam Sivam Sundaram*, Vol. 1 (Prasanthi Nilayam, India: Sri Sathya Sai Books & Publications Trust, n.d.), 10-11.

5 Erlendur Haraldsson, Ph.D., *Modern Miracles – An Investigative Report on Psychic Phenomena Associated with Sathya Sai Baba* (Mamaroneck, NY: Hastings House, 1997), 85.

6 Kasturi, *Sathyam*, 156.

7 "A Conversation with Sri Sathya Sai Baba," communication from saidevotees_worldnet@yahoogroups.com, April 1, 2008. The conversation occurred many years ago and first appeared in the official ashram magazine.

8 Dr. John S. Hislop, *My Baba and I* (Prasanthi Nilayam, India: Sri Sathya Sai Books & Publications Trust, n.d.), 205-06.

9 "A Conversation with Sri Sathya Sai Baba."

first SELF,
then help

ॐ

"Swami, what is the root of all chaos and trouble in the world today?"

What we think we do not speak, what we speak we do not act, what we act we do not mean, what we actually mean, we never think about in the first place. What is the world? . . . . It is the reflection of your own self. When there is chaos within your own self, how can you find tranquility outside? Otherwise, everything outside is in perfect harmony. The sun, the moon, the wind, everything follows nature's laws. Only human beings break the laws of nature and suffer. The discontentment and disharmony in one's own self get projected outside as chaos. Set your own Self in order, and you will find everything outside in order.

Once you know yourself, everything else will be automatically clear . . . . Just as the knowledge of a single clay pot is enough to know about all clay pots, when you know yourself, all else can be known.

First, SELF; then help; improve yourself, teach yourself, reconstruct yourself, and then proceed to solve the problems of others. That reconstruction is quite easy, provided you inquire calmly into your own personality.

To rectify the world and put it on the proper path, we have to first rectify ourselves and our conduct.

We light many candles with the flame of a single candle. But remember only a burning candle can light other candles. An unlit candle cannot light other unlit candles. Only one who has earned wisdom can enlighten others who are in ignorance. One who is himself unillumined cannot illumine others dwelling in the darkness, Maya. One must light his own lamp from the universal light of love and thence forward he can transmit illumination to all who seek and strive. All lamps shine alike since they are all sparks of . . . the Universal Luminosity that is God.

There are certain dire possibilities which I want all social workers to guard against. First cleanse your own minds and then start advising others. Earn mental peace and strength for yourself and then try to secure them for others. Learn the secret of lasting happiness yourself and then endeavor to make others happy. Seek the real limb not the artificial limb. Get the doctor who will assure "hereafter you will not fall ill" and not the doctor who gives some relief only for the present attack.

The Indispensable ⋐⋑

Mark Van Doren was a professor of English at Columbia University, 1942–59. Some students asked him what they should do with their lives, and he answered, "Whatever you want, just so long as you do not miss the main thing." And what was that, someone asked. "Your own lives," he said.

DC J (Fadiman, *Anecdotes*, 560)

Learning all about external things without knowing your real self is like studying the branches of a tree, ignoring its roots. There are many fruits on the tree. We can see the fruits. What happens if you water those fruits? They will fall down. But if you water the roots down below, the tree flourishes and will give fruits which can be enjoyed. You have to develop self-knowledge and self-confidence and then only can you help others.

One does not have to search for spiritual power, going around the world and spending a lot of money. Be in your own house, develop it in yourself! Such spiritual power is in you. You do not have to run for it here and there. God is not external; God is not outside you; God is inside you . . . . Do not be under the delusion that God is somewhere and you have to search for him.

The idea of search is an error. Everyone already knows the truth. All that is needed is to put that truth into practice, to manifest it.

One should not be concerned only about one's own welfare, career and prosperity. It is not for the enjoyment of personal possessions and comforts that man has taken birth. He has a greater goal to be achieved, something more permanent and lasting. It is the realization of oneness with the Divine, which alone can give lasting bliss. Even while being engaged in the activities of the secular world, we should strive to sanctify all actions by dedicating them to the Divine.

Man is endowed with unlimited powers. Not a single man is without them. But the road is missed, since he is unaware of this truth.

Divinity is present in man like fragrance in a flower, fire in wood and oil in sesamum, not visible but latent. Unaware of this inner truth, men are carried away by external appearances and consider them as the reality.

The Musk deer runs frantically in its search for the fragrance that fascinates it. When at last, it is too exhausted to continue, it discovers that the source of that fragrance has been within its own self all along! So too, man searches in vain for Ananda [bliss] in the outside world, only to realize in the end that it has been within his own Self!

In our daily experiences, there are a number of instances which reveal the existence of Divinity in every person. Consider a cinema; on the screen we see rivers in flood, engulfing all the surrounding land. Even though the scene is filled with floodwaters the screen does not get wet by even a drop of water. At another time, on the same screen we see volcanoes erupting with tongues of flame, but the screen is not burnt. The screen which provides the basis for all these pictures is not affected by any of them. Likewise in the life of man, good or bad, joy or sorrow, birth or death, will be coming and going, but they do not affect the *Atma*. In the cinema of life the screen is the *Atma* . . . . it is divinity.

Man is empowered with limitless, latent abilities, which will manifest themselves at the appropriate moment. Every devotee has these unseen and unknown abilities. Man contains within himself all the powers and all the substances that exist anywhere in the cosmos.

The *Atma* is the unseen basis, the substance of all the objective world, the reality behind the appearance, universal and immanent in every being. **It is inherently devoid of attachment, is imperishable and does not die. It is the witness, unaffected by all this change in time and space, the immanent spirit in the body, the motivating force of its impulses and intentions. It is one's own innermost reality, one's divinity, the real self – the soul.**

The *Atma* cannot be grasped through metaphors and examples. No form can contain it; no name can denote it. **How can the limited comprehend the unlimited**; the now measure the ever; the wayward understand the stable?

The *Atma* persists unchanged, however many changes the thing motivated by it might undergo. It contacts the senses of perception and affects the mind; it awakens the intellect to discriminate and decide upon the lines of action. It activates the instruments of thought, speech and action, of expression and communication. The eyes see, but what force prompts them? You may have ears, but who endows them with the power of hearing? Words emanate from the mouth, but what urges us and frames the manner and content of the speech? That force acts like the cells in a torch which provide the bulb with the current to illuminate it. Doctors know that the body consists of cells, billions of them, alive and alert, busy and active. Each cell is motivated by the *Atma*; it is immanent, all over. The *Atma* is in each of them, as well as in every spot of space. **When we realize it as such, it is experienced as effulgent, total, splendorous light: endless, incomparable, unique light.** *

---

* All emphases are from Sai Baba's original quotations.

Some laugh at spiritual aspirants and call them idle visionaries who are seeking something that is not tangible, that cannot be weighed and valued! The unseen is the basis of the seen. You do not see your breath or weigh it, but breath is the very sustenance of life.

Cultivate a nearness with me in the heart and it will be rewarded. Then you, too, will acquire a fraction of that supreme love. This is a great chance. Be confident that you will all be liberated. Know that you are saved. Many hesitate to believe that things will improve, that life will be happy for all and full of joy, and that the golden age will recur. Let me assure you that this divine body has not come in vain. It will succeed in averting the crisis that has come upon humanity.

My Birthday is the Date when Divinity Blossoms in your Heart. (Nov. 23)

Essentials

☙

Spirit

No society can find its fulfillment, no social ideal can fructify, without the blossoming of the spirit of man.

Almost always, man is anxious to ignore the faults and failings of the objects that draw his attention. If he only recognizes these he is certain to evaluate them correctly and behave more intelligently. When a man becomes aware that the cobra is a poisonous snake and that the leopard is a cruel beast, he avoids them with constant vigilance. Similarly, when we become aware of the transitoriness and triviality of worldly triumphs and possessions, we can easily detach ourselves from them and concentrate on inner wealth and inner vision. All things in the outer world of objects are subject to change. Impermanent objects can confer only impermanent happiness to man who is himself impermanent. How can it ever be otherwise? Only the spring of bliss can confer bliss. A fitful spring, a drying, decaying spring, can give happiness only in fits, and even that will, before long, decay and dry.

Atma alone is the ever-full and ever-fresh spring of bliss. The atmic energy motivates every being in the universe – man, animal, bird, worm, tree and grass. Once man contacts it, he is blessed with universal vision, absolute delight and eternal wisdom. Everyone has the thirst to realize it and be with it, but very few take steps to reach it. Thousands proclaim the glory of the *Atma*, but only a handful strive to attain it.

Does the key exist in the outer world or in the inner? So long as man embroils himself in the "seen," he cannot see the "see-er." So long as his attention is caught by the flowers in the garland, he cannot recognize the string that holds them together. Inquiry is essential to discover the base which upholds the garland. So too, inquiry alone can bring into human experience the atmic base which upholds the objective sensory world.

God is neither distant nor distinct from you.

To search for God as something different from you is a delusion.

Do not think that you are human and that you have to reach the state of the Divine. **Think rather than you are God, and from that state you have become a human being.** As you think this way, all the attributes of God will manifest in you. Know that you have descended from God as human beings and that eventually you will go back to your source.

Determination

If you do not have the quality of determination, then patience will have no basis and cannot develop in strength. Patience and determination are twins: one cannot exist without the other. Without determination, patience cannot establish itself, and without patience, determination will degenerate into arrogance.

Without firm determination, no great thing can be achieved in life.

Do not waver, hesitate or doubt your destiny.

Delight

Joy is your birthright; peace is your inmost nature.

Man is seeking joy in far-off places, in quiet spots, not knowing that the spring of joy is in his heart, the haven of peace is in himself.

Deep Concentration

To the doubting or confused ones, I give this illustration. Those who want to secure pearls from the sea have to dive deep to fetch them. It does not help them to dabble among the shallow waves near the shore and say that the sea has no pearls and all stories about them are false.

Self-Inquiry

Self-examination is the first step to self-improvement and peace.

In all your spiritual practices that you engage in, you should **spend three-quarters of your time** on Self-inquiry; then you will get the full results.

Instead of criticizing others and finding faults with the actions of others, subject yourself to vigilant scrutiny, understand yourself well, and correct your own faults. Do not be like the dancer who blamed the drummer for her wrong steps.

Self-Trust

Believe in yourself, first. Then believe in the Lord.

The first thing to do is to acquire confidence in yourself. Today self-confidence has completely disappeared amongst the students. It is only when you have self-confidence that you will have self-satisfaction. When a small bird perches on a small branch of a tree, on account of the weight of the bird, that branch shakes, but the bird is not going to be upset by such a movement. What is the reason? The bird which is sitting on the branch is not depending for its safety on the branch. It is depending on its own wings. Even if the branch moves up and down or even if the branch breaks, because the bird is depending on its own wings, it can fly away. It does not worry at all. Even the small bird which is sitting on the branch has got so much confidence in its own wings and in itself that it is fearless.

Without self-confidence no achievement is possible. If you have confidence in your strength and skill, you can draw upon the inner springs of courage and raise yourselves to a higher level of joy and peace. For confidence in yourselves arises through the *Atma*, which is your inner reality. The *Atma* is peace, it is joy, it is strength, it is wisdom. So it is from the *Atma* that you draw all these equipments for spiritual progress.

Faith in yourself and faith in God are identical; you tap the strength of God within when you stand at attention against an enemy without.

It does not matter a bit if you have no faith in ME or in God. Have faith in yourself. That is enough. For who are you really? Each of you is Divinity, whether you know it or not.

Self-Loyalty

Let the mountains fall; let the sea overwhelm the land; but do not give up your Sadhana (spiritual practice).

Act according to your professions. Do not play false to yourself and to your ideals. To deny by your acts the truth of what you preach is a sign of cowardice and moral suicide.

Love

The best spiritual discipline that can help man is love. Foster the tiny seed of love that clings to "me" and "mine"; let it sprout into love for the group around you and grow into love for all mankind and spread out its branches over animals, birds, and those that creep and crawl, and let the love enfold all things and beings in all the world. Proceed from less love to more love, narrow love to expanded love.

Love is central. Love in thought is truth – that which is always the same and beyond beginning and end. **Love in feeling is peace, bliss – being unaffected by the sorrows or joys, the ups or downs in life. Love in understanding is non-violence and respect and reverence for all creation. Love in action is morality and right living** – the giving of selfless service to all in need without desire for reward.

Vision

The inextricable connection between the phenomenal world outside and the world of consciousness inside eludes the understanding of ordinary people. Immersed in the desire for enjoying worldly pleasures, they do not attempt to discover the boundless joy to be derived from the inner Spirit. This is because all the sense organs are open only to experiences from outside.... Only a few develop the inner vision and enjoy spiritual bliss.

Change your Vision and the world will appear accordingly. Let the eye be charged with the Divine, it will see all as God. It is foolish to try to shape the World; shape yourself as the embodiment of Peace, Love and Reverence. Then you will see all as Love, Compassion and Humility.

Humility

Do not believe that mastery of many TOMES makes you wise. Wisdom can grow only where humility prevails.

Character

A life without character is as barren as a temple without a lamp, a coin that is counterfeit, a kite whose string has snapped.

The manner of living is more important than the standard of living.

Destiny

Each man carries his destiny in his own hands.

    You have it in your power to make your days on Earth a path of flowers, instead of thorns.

Teachers

◌

Swami had two shirts and pants to last a year. There was no money even for a pin, thorns were used to hold torn places together. Tears in the cloth came from schoolmates who would punish Baba for always knowing the answers at school. Only he would know the answer. If he gave the answer, the boys would beat him. If he did not give it, the teacher would beat him. On some occasions, the pupil who answered had to slap the faces of those who did not. Since Swami was small, he had to stand on a chair to slap. But he would slap gently. Then the teacher would slap him hard as many times as he had slapped gently. Of course [then] the boys . . . would be loving and affectionate to Baba.

(Baba, telling Dr. Hislop)

When you reach the bank of a river in a strange land, you do not take advice from a lame person or a blind person on where you can best wade across. You follow a person who has waded often and who is neither lame nor blind. The man who can see is a scholar; the man who can walk is a person with experience. The man with both capacities is a good guide, not those who prattle things learnt from the books or dole out set formulae irrespective of the stage the recipient has reached, or roam about in search of people whom they can squeeze for money.

A man struggling in a bog cannot be saved by another who is also caught in its slime. Only one standing on the firm ground can pull him out. So the guru must have a secure footing above and beyond the slush of worldly life.

How can a person who cannot swim, teach others the art? How can one whose granary is empty, pour out charity? Acquire the wealth of devotion, fortitude and peace, before venturing to advise others how to acquire them.

Teachers are reservoirs from which, through the process of education, students draw the water of life.

There are three kinds of teachers – those who complain, complain, complain; those who explain, explain, explain; and those who inspire.

There is a way of life, a method of uplift, a path of progress, distinct for every seeker, different from those of others. The true guru knows which suits you best.

All That Counts ❧

"Some years ago—I'm sure they order these things better now—I had occasion to visit the kindergarten class of a highly progressive school, attended by my small son Jonathon. The tots were engaged in what I believe is termed rhythmic play. They were following the lead of their teacher, an energetic young woman, who danced and marched about the room clapping her hands in time to the music of a phonograph record. The docile pupils straggled along behind her in somewhat ragged formation.

"After the rhythmic play was over, I drew my five-year-old son Jonathon aside—his countenance had seemed particularly knowing and stoical—and said: 'I guess you have lots of fun doing that, don't you?' He turned his face up to me and replied, with philosophic resignation: 'No, we don't, but'—he pointed to the teacher—'she does.'"

Clifton Fadiman

(Fadiman, Anecdotes, 224.)

Do not confine your studies to this circle and these books. The Universe is the University for you. You can imbibe wisdom from the sky, the clouds, the mountains, the rivers, the daily phenomena of sunrise and sunset, the season, the birds, trees, flowers, insects – in fact all beings and things in the universe. Approach these teachers with awe, reverence and humility; they will respond with lessons.

What profit is it for the children to know the length of the Mississippi River or the height of Vesuvius? Why load them with information they may never require? On the other hand, give them the tonic to strengthen their spirit.... Now, they sing, "Ding dong bell, Pussy is in the well." This type of silly meaningless jargon is spreading everywhere like a poisonous infection, destroying the seeds of peace and joy.

God is the echo of the hills, the flutter of the leaves, the whisper of men, the babble of children, the OM that is wafted everywhere. There is nothing except God. **Nature is his manifestation.** Man must recognize God in all human beings and in all else that exists. **God is in everyone and in everything.**

The study of the mind and the science of perfecting consciousness has not developed because man seeks peace and joy in external things and objective pleasures. The attention all along has been on the outer senses and methods by which they can be used to collect information and pleasurable experiences. The vast regions of inner consciousness have been left fallow . . . .

Man has all the capabilities in him, but he is unaware of his glory; he knows only a faction of his power, and even that faintly and falteringly. He is degrading himself by yielding to three temptations: physical, worldly and scholastic. The scholastic temptation attracts people who are learned; it prompts them into controversy and competitive exhibitionism and ruins them by bloating their ego. The worldly temptation leads man to seek cheap renown and gain fame and favor through all means available. The physical temptation insists on beautifying the body and resorts to measures which will hide the oncoming of age.

Avatars seldom give advice directly. Whenever they wish to communicate, they convey more often by way of indirect suggestions and only rarely by direct method of instruction. The reason for this is there is divinity inherent in every human being, which he can manifest spontaneously if favourable conditions are provided, just as a viable seed will germinate and grow into a tree because of its inherent nature, if only suitable facilities are provided for the manifestation of its potentiality. Man should be enabled to correct himself by his own efforts, by merely giving timely suggestions rather than by stultifying his freedom and dignity through directives imposed from without. In short, the best maxim for helping people either in worldly matters or in the spiritual field is: *"Help them to help themselves"* or *"Self-help is the best help."*

Being and Doing

∽

The Call

I want that you all should build new houses for happy living and install the Lord therein. I do not mean houses of brick and mortar, but houses of good thoughts, good words, good deeds and good company, where you could live calm and collected.

Begin to perceive your inner voice and follow it.

The lights have to be switched on in the heart of man, rather than in the house where the image of the Lord is installed and worshipped.

All spiritual practice must be directed to the removal of the husk and the revelation of the kernel.

Choice

Man must first decide, after vigorous self-examination, the path that he wishes to traverse.

It is best to live with honor for just a day than with dishonor for many decades; better a short-lived celestial swan than a century-lived crow.

Listening and Remembering

Today, man has developed a disease in his hearing. Many people give their ears to all types of spiritual discourses, but that doesn't mean they're seeking the maximum benefit from listening. Many satisfy themselves by saying that it is enough to merely listen. This sort of confidence, this kind of approach, is not proper. We listen to Swami's discourses for a long time and derive a great deal of happiness by merely listening. But the real question is – are we able to put into practice anything that we have heard? If not, then we can conclude that the sense of hearing is becoming diseased. In addition to hearing we have to develop the faculty of thinking of what we have heard, and consider what is good and useful about it – and then put into practice the good things that we have heard. Nothing will be achieved if we merely listen and don't think about or do . . . .

Take, for example, what is happening now in this hall. We are all seated and listening to Swami. But after listening, you'll leave the hall and forget. What kind of an attitude is this? What kind of confidence in Swami's teaching is this? If you immediately forget, then what a waste of time it is for all of us! What an effort has been wasted on Swami's part! Think of what you are asking of Swami, the kind of spiritual gift you wish to receive from me. Do you

have confidence – are you willing to give the kind of attention and practice needed to achieve your dream? Only
when you think about what you have heard, and put it into
practice – at least one or two of the items that Swami is
talking about – only then will you be consecrating your life
and finding some meaning in your life by coming here.

Forgetting

Forget the harm that anyone has done to you, and
forget the good that you have done to others.

Action and Application

Knowledge without action is useless, and action without knowledge is dangerous.

Knowledge that is not put into practice is like food that is not digested.

The important thing is not to give up the action, but the fruits of the action.... Hence, work or service is to be done without the desire for rewards or return.

Whatever acts a good or bad man may do, the fruits thereof follow him and will never stop pursuing him.

Condemn the wrong and extol the right as soon as you notice either in your children; that will settle them on the straight path.

The Acid Test

The acid test by which an activity can be confirmed as holy or sacred is to examine whether it promotes attachment or avoids bondage.

Self-Faith

Only those who have faith in themselves shall have faith in God.

When the sun is over your head, there will be no shadow; similarly, when faith is steady in your head, it should not cast any shadow of doubt.

Have faith in yourself. When you have no faith in the wave, how can you get faith in the ocean?

Self-Reliance

Be self-reliant, self-confident, see through your own eyes; hear through your own ears. Most people today believe their ears and deny their eyes; or they use the eyes, ears and even the brains of others, and thus fall into error and fear.

Don't deny the validity of your own experience. Stand on your strength, be unmoved either by adulation or denigration. Follow my lead. I am unaffected by either. I march on alone, undeterred and of my own accord. I am my own guide and witness, have full faith in this.

Steadfastness

Whether others esteem you or not, you must commit to act according to your conscience. The inner conviction that you are acting right is your best witness.

Intensity

Spiritual Exercises: The more intensity, the greater the results.

What is the basic factor that prevents us from having that right experience of light and wisdom?

We don't have the intensity that is required. Even to study books how much is needed to come to the stage when we can read difficult books? How many years, how many hours of toil we put into it. If you have the same intensity in spiritual practice, you will surely know the truth. But we are not as intense as we should be on the spiritual path. We do not apply a one-pointedness. Full concentration is needed even in the world in walking, talking, reading. Without concentration you cannot do anything. Even in little things of the world we use concentration.

But when we try to think of God, then we get restless, and the mind is unstable. Why do we do the things of the world with full concentration? Why? Because we are fully interested in it. And with God we have these doubts.

Whatever work you love deeply, you have full concentration. Whatever you don't love deeply, then concentration is not full. A small example: You are driving a car. At the same time you are talking to your passengers. The road becomes narrow and dangerous. You say, "Please let us not talk now, I must give full concentration to the driving." Why do you say this? It is because you deeply love your life and must concentrate deeply so as to avoid an accident.

Because you have this love for body, you concentrate on its safety. When you have deep love for God, then concentration on Him will come automatically.

Discipline

The boulder on the hill, from which a portion has been blasted away to carve an idol for the temple, tells the idol, "Thath Thawam Asi" (You and I are the same), That and this are one substance. Yes, of one substance, but what a difference. The hammer and chisel have made one, a thing of beauty and a joy forever, an inspiration to make life beautiful and holy. You too must subject yourself to the hammer of discipline and the chisel of pain-pleasure, so that you become Divine.

Discipline is the mark of intelligent living.

Discrimination

You must take every step in Sadhana (spiritual practice) or in Samsara (the sensory world) only after deep deliberation and satisfying yourself that it will be for your good. Otherwise, it will be like the story of the weeping city. One day, a close female attendant of the Queen came to the palace weeping in great sorrow, and so the Queen began to shed tears. Seeing the Queen in tears, the entire [servant body] wept and the weeping spread to the male attendants also. The King, finding the Queen inconsolably sad, also wept profusely in sympathy, and the sight made the entire city weep loudly without end. At last, one sensible person set in motion an inquiry, which passed through person after person until the Queen herself was accosted. She said that her attendant was in sore grief, and when she, a washer-woman by caste, was interrogated, she confessed that it was all due to the sudden demise of her favorite ass. Reason out; discriminate; and do not rush to conclusion or be led away by mere hearsay.

Meditation

It is best you stay away from companions who drag you to such distractions that weaken and worry you; spend a few minutes every morning and evening in the silence of your own home, spend them with the highest of all powers that you know of; be in His Elevating and Inspiring Company; worship Him mentally; offer unto Him all the work you do; and you will come out of the silence, nobler and more heroic than when you went in.

Whenever and wherever you put yourself in touch with God, that is the state of meditation.

Practice Silence: For the Voice of God can be heard in the region of your heart only when the tongue is still.

You toil day and night for this world; how many minutes do you devote for the master of the world?

Meditation is constant inner inquiry as to who am "I," what is loving, and what is harsh.

Company of the Good

Seek the company of the good, the seekers, the aspirants, the detached. Then you will see the light. Listen to the holy discourses, read sacred books. Your effort and the atmosphere of the place, these two will lead you to success. The place has a subtle and powerful influence on man. Holy place, holy river, holy company, holy day, when these conjoin, it is the chance of a lifetime; make fullest use of it.

The eye which is scarcely two inches long can see millions of miles into space but is incapable of seeing itself! Man too is as shrewd and as weak as the eye. He can analyze others' motives, count others' faults and map out others' skills and capacities, but he is powerless to analyze himself, his feelings and his emotions. Unwilling to discover his own faults, he cannot assess his innate skill and realize his inner reality! But the power can be acquired if you keep company with Sadhakas (spiritual aspirants), not otherwise.

Ascetic practices, years of constant recitation of the name [of God], pilgrimages to holy places and shrines, study of sacred books – these will not help the aspirant to spiritual victory as much as communion with the godly and good.

Seeing the Good

The purpose of all Sadhana (spiritual practice) is to see the good, the Divine in everything and to be able to overlook the bad, the evil. From the viewpoint of Divinity, there is no good or bad – all is Divine. But the mind sees this as good and that as bad, this as right and that as wrong. It is the mind that must be trained to see the Divine in everyone and in each difficulty.

A small example: a dead dog is on the road, crows are pecking at it. People walk by and say, "Oh, what a terrible sight and horrible smell!" But Jesus was walking by and He said, "What beautiful teeth the dog has, so white and shiny. Nobody was brushing or taking care, but still the dog kept such beautiful teeth." Jesus was showing that one can see the best qualities in even the worst situations. People who are saintly look always to the good and do not become entangled in the bad.

Equality

There may be differences among men, in physical strength, financial status, intellectual acumen – but all are equal in the eye of God.

You are all separate beads strung together on that one thread, God.

Love

A revolution – more powerful and pervasive than any that man has undergone so far – neither political, economic, scientific nor technological, but deeper and more basic, is now on. It is the Spiritual Revolution; the revolution has love as both its means and end. It will awaken the springs of love all over the world in the fields of education, morality, law, politics, commerce and science.

The purpose of the ancient religions of India is to plant the seeds of love in the human heart, so that they may sprout into saplings of endurance, and blossom into tolerance, yielding ultimately the fruit of peace. The pinnacle of Indian thought is non-duality, experience of the One, negation of duality. Some countries proceed toward the ideal of individual freedom, others aim at state sovereignty and the suppression of the individual's right to freedom. But Bharat [the land of Godward activity] has, from time immemorial, sought to infuse in the individual the conviction that he can be free only when he realizes his identity with all – not only with the inhabitants of his own state, or people who use his language or are of his own colour and creed. Expansion is the key to happiness, and love is the unfailing key to expansion.

Prema (love) is the greatest spiritual activity. *Prema* is not mere reciprocal love. It is an extended and sublimated form of self-love. It is an extension of love to humanity and to the entire creation.

The most important thing you have to develop is love. If you develop love, you don't have to develop anything else.

The Grace of God cannot be won through the gymnasium of reason, the contortions of yoga or the denials of asceticism. Love alone can win it, Love that needs no requital, Love that knows no bargaining, Love that is unwavering. Love alone can overcome obstacles, however many or mighty.

Love binds all hearts in a soft silken symphony. Seen through the eyes of love, all beings are beautiful, all deeds are dedicated, all thoughts are innocent, [and] the world is one vast kin.

There is only one caste, the caste of Humanity;
There is only one religion, the religion of Love;
There is only one language, the language of the Heart.

Love is the only wealth that does not diminish. It is the property of God. Therefore, cultivate pure and selfless love. God's love will always follow you wherever you are and will protect you at all times. Do not ever consider that money alone constitutes your wealth. In fact, love is your real wealth. The wealth of love always grows; it never diminishes. Only those who realize the principle of love will be able to understand this truth.

Cultivate . . . love; that will save you, for all the service that you do to others through that love is in fact service done to yourself. It is not the others that you help, it is yourself that is helped, remember.

Love should not be rationed on the basis of caste, creed, economic status, or the intellectual attainment of the recipient. It should flow full and free regardless of the consequences, for it is one's nature to love – to seek out the dry, dreary wastes which love can water and make fertile. Wherever there is a vacuum in any heart, love flows into it and is glad that it can fill the emptiness. It is never held back; it is offered in abundance without guile or deceit; it does not wear the cloak of flattery, falsehood, or fear. The tendrils of love aspire to cling only to the garments of God. They sense that God, in His Infinite Splendor, resides in every heart, and so probe silently into the innermost recess of all personalities around so that they may bloom therein. That is true devotion of love of God . . . .

Love must see the best in others and not the worst. Love cannot ignore the divinity in others. The greatest of the virtues is love.

Self is love-less-ness; love is self-less-ness. Self gets and forgets; love gives and forgives. Love can never entertain the idea of revenge, for it sees all others as oneself. When the tongue is hurt by the teeth, do you seek vengeance against the wrong-doer?

Soft, sweet speech is the expression of genuine love. Hate screeches, fear squeals, conceit trumpets. But love sings lullabies, it soothes, it applies balm. Practice the vocabulary of love, and unlearn the language of hate and contempt.

Do not give all your thoughts immediate expression; select, ponder, and then speak out. Speak softly, sweetly, without malice in your heart; speak as if you are addressing the Sai who resides in everyone.

Do not withhold the sweet word, the supporting hand, the assuring smile, the comforting company, the consoling conversation.

There will be no temptation for others to shout when you talk to them in whispers.

Have constructive thoughts, consoling words, compas-
sionate acts. Be on the look-out for eyes filled with tears,
hearts heaving in sighs.

Shower cheer on the sad; soothe those that have lost
the way; close your eyes to the faults of others, but keep
them open to discover your own.

Scatter the seeds of love in dreary desert hearts; then
sprouts of love will make wastelands green with joy; blossoms of love will make the air fragrant; rivers of love will
murmur along the valleys, and every bird will beat, every
child will sing the song of love.

Tactful Love ∝

Joseph Hodges Choate was the American ambassador to Great Britain, 1899–1905, a superb speaker and wit.

"Who would you like to be if you were not yourself?" someone asked him at a private dinner.

Choate skimmed a list in mind of the rich and the famous, past and present, then eyeing his wife, replied, "If I could not be myself, I would like to be Mrs. Choate's second husband."

DCJ (Fadiman, Anecdotes, 118)

There is no living being without the spark of love; even a mad man loves something or somebody.

Have the Love of God filling and thrilling your heart; then, you cannot hate anyone.

Learn this lesson of light and love; move out, clasp, spread, expand, give up limits of mine and thine, his and theirs, caste and creed, in one limitless flow of love.

Love is God, God is love. Where there is love, there God is certainly evident. Love more and more people. Love them more and more intensely. Transform the love into service. Transform the service into worship. That is the highest spiritual discipline.

Duty without love is deplorable. Duty with love is desirable. Love without duty is Divine. Duty implies force or compulsion while love is spontaneous and expresses itself without external promptings.

Love expresses itself as service. Love grows through service. Love is born in the womb of service.

What is the unmistakable mark of a wise man?
It is love, love for all humanity.

Hislop: What is the art of looking whereby one may see the Lord even in unpleasant and disagreeable persons?

Even in persons of unpleasant nature, be aware that the Lord is in the heart even of that person. Have that aspect in mind and treat the person from that viewpoint to the best of your ability. In time that person will respond, and his nature will change.

Hislop: How does one see God Himself?

In order to see the moon, does one need a torch? It is by the light of the moon that one sees the moon. In like fashion, if one wishes to see God, it is by love, which is the light of God, that one may see Him.

Gratitude

You may be able to pay back any debt; but the debt you owe your mother, you never can repay.

Happiness

Happiness is essential for God-realization. It is one of the major gates to divinity. It is not just a fault if a person is not happy; it is one of the most serious of all faults. It is a barrier to Realization.

Patience

Patience is all the strength that man needs.

Oneness

The mind fixed in the awareness of the One is like a rock, unaffected by doubt, stable, secure.

Cultivate that attitude of Oneness between men of all creeds, all countries and all continents.

Love of the country is the basis on which you can build love for the world community.

Each country is but a room in the mansion of God.

One with the Energies

Matter in all forms is only energy.... Scientists only work on the external source of energy, they don't investigate the internal sources. You go millions of miles into space, but you don't go half-an-inch within where lies your strength...

Joy and peace do not inhere in external objects; they are in yourself.

Perfection

It is a grievous error to think that it is natural for man to err.

Practice alone makes man perfect.

Genius and Perfection ❧

Genius is an outcropping of the infinite powers of humanity. When he was two, Mozart was taken to a farm where he heard a pig squeal. "G-sharp!" he cried. Someone dashed to a piano, and G-sharp it was.

DCJ (Fadiman, Anecdotes, 415)

Service

People often think they have to be perfect themselves before they can help anyone else, but such is not the case.

The services to man are more valuable than what you call "Services to God." God has no need of your service. Please man; you please God.

But do not believe that you can by means of service reform or reshape the world. You may or you may not. That does not matter. The real value of service, its most visible result, is that it reforms you, reshapes you.

Learn a lesson from the tree. When it is heavy with fruits, it does not raise its head aloft in pride, it bends low, stoops, as if it does not take any credit for its accomplishment and as if it helps you to pluck the fruit. Learn a lesson from the birds. They feed those who cannot fly far. The bird relieves the itch of the buffalo by scratching it with its beak; they help and serve each other with no thought of reward. How much more alert must man be then with his superior skills and faculties? Service is the best cure for egoism.

The Chakora bird waits with open beak for the first drops of the very first rain that comes from the sky; it relishes no other. So too, you should yearn for the chance to console, comfort, encourage, heal, help, someone looking for it. See yourself in him; feel his joy to be yours, his sorrow to be yours.

There was a king once, who questioned many a scholar and sage who came to his court, "Which is the best service and which is the best time to render it?" He could not get a satisfying answer from them. One day while pursuing the forces of a rival king, he got separated from his troops, until he reached a hermitage. There was an old monk who received him kindly and offered him a welcome cup of cool water. After a little rest the king asked his host the question that was tormenting his brain: "Which is the best service?" The hermit said, "Giving a thirsty man a cup of water." "And, which is the best time to render it?" The answer was, "When he comes far and lonely, looking for some place where he can get it." The act of service is not to be judged, according to the cost or publicity it entails; it may be only the offering of a cup of water in the depth of a jungle. But the need of the recipient, the mood of the person who offers – these decide whether the act is gold or lead.

If you pour spirituality into the ears of those who are tortured by hunger, it will not be assimilated. First, quench the hunger.

Give them God in the form of food.

Give them God in the form of clothes.

Give God in the form of peace to those who are afflicted with anxiety.

Give God in the form of medicine to those who are suffering from ill-health.

Give God in whatever form will assuage fear, pain and sorrow.

It is only after this is done that spirituality can soak into the heart. If you act contrariwise, instead of spiritual feelings, you will be promoting atheism itself.

Being a good example is the best form of service.

He who dedicates his time, skill and strength to Service will never meet with defeat, distress or disappointment, for Service is its own reward.

Efforts to serve must spring from agony at the suffering of others, and the service must be the genuine effort to get rid of that anguish. And...do not worry about the result. Help as much as you can, as efficiently as you can, as silently as you can, as lovingly as you can. Leave the rest to God, who gave you the chance to serve.

Service should not be exhibitionistic; you must seek no reward, not even gratitude or thanks from the recipients.

Service is spiritual discipline, not a pastime of the rich and well-placed.

Do not serve for the sake of reward, attracting attention, or earning gratitude, or from a sense of pride at your superiority in skill, wealth, status or authority. Serve because you are urged by Love.

It is so easy for the poor to stay poor, to eat with the poor and lay with the poor and continue to take on the suffering and problems of the poor. And it's so easy for the rich to be with the rich and eat with the rich and play with the rich and forget about the poor. It is very uncommon and very difficult for the rich to live with the poor, to eat with the poor, to take on the problems and suffering of the poor. But this is what I'm telling you to do. Go to the poor, live with the poor, be with the poor, the helpless, the suffering, and serve them.

Service to children is the most sacred.

Do not imagine that your service to children is just for their sake. It is equally so for your own sake.

Equality

How are all equal? Because they have all the same consciousness within them. When the sun rises, not all lotuses in the lake bloom; only the grown buds open their petals. The others await their chance. It is the same with men. Differences do exist because of unripeness, though all fruits have to ripen and fall some day. Every being has to reach the goal however slow they walk or however curved their road.

Kings and Servants ଔ

Alexander the Great once noticed the philosopher Diogenes scrutinizing a pile of human bones.

"What are you looking for?" he asked.

"I am looking for the bones of your father," answered Diogenes, "but I cannot distinguish them from those of his slaves."

DC J (Fadiman, Anecdotes, 169)

Calm

Peace is what everyone seeks; but it can never be secured from the outside world. Accumulation of riches, or power, cannot endow peace. Peace can only come from the fountain of peace within.

Once you enter the depths of the sea, it is all calm, it is all peace. Agitation, noise, confusion – all are only on the outer layers. So also in the innermost recesses of the heart, there is a reservoir of peace where you must take refuge.

When you have attained true wisdom, you will find that good fortune should not be gloated over, nor bad fortune be grieved over.

Without being at peace with yourselves, you cannot be at peace with others.

If you are at peace with yourself, you will discern peace all around.

Peace descends like dew.

Equanimity

However high a bird may soar, it has sooner or later to perch on a treetop, to enjoy quiet.

By not getting excited over the angry words of a critic, one becomes superior to the critic. Otherwise, one descends to the same level as the critic.

What makes you think that "doing" is so important? Be equal-minded. Then you will not be bothered about "doing" or "not doing," success or failure; the balance will remain unaffected by either. Let the wave of memory, the storm of desire, the fire of emotion pass through without affecting your equanimity. Be a witness of these. Commitment engenders holding, narrowing, limiting. Be willing to be nothing. Let all dualities subside in your neutrality.

Humor

My name is Sathya, truth. I represent that which is beyond mind. I have come to show you who you are – the reality that lies beyond mind. How can a scientist comprehend me? I am all places at all times – everything that ever was or will be. I can transmute the earth into sky and the sky into earth... [pausing with a sparkle] But I don't do it often because it causes inconvenience to some people.

Humor in Hard Times ❧

Charlie Grimm managed the Chicago Cubs, with little success in later years. One time a scout phoned him from the boonies, raving about a new Moses.

"Charlie," he exclaimed, "I've landed the greatest young pitcher in the land. He struck out every man who came to bat — twenty-seven in a row. Nobody even got a foul until two were out in the ninth. The pitcher is right here with me. What shall I do?"

Said Grimm, "Sign up the guy who got the foul. We're looking for hitters."

DC J (Fadiman, Anecdotes, 258)

Warnings

Education is being confused with the acquisition of verbal scholarship. This is wrong. Education must open the doors of the mind. Many describe science today as a powerful acquisition, but science holds before mankind a great opportunity, that is all. It cannot be as great a power as it is imagined to be. If it is **devoid of character, it brings disaster** .... Intelligence can be found to be very high among clever thieves. So, too, scientific knowledge can be misused for destructive purposes.

To enter Heaven, man must transform himself into an innocent infant. This is the Truth. To enter the Heaven of science, man has to mould himself into a humble, unselfish seeker.

Be sincere; talk only about your genuine experience; do not distort, exaggerate or falsify that experience.

Do not be misled by the belief of the existence of two entities: this world and the next, here and hereafter; this world is interwoven with the next.

Instead of making the senses which are at best very poor guides and informants his servants, man has made them his masters.

I am not for indiscriminate reading of books however valuable they may be. Much reading tends to confuse the mind. It fosters argumentation and intellectual pride. What I insist upon is putting the things read into practice, if not all, at least a thing or two. Moreover, remember that a book is only a pointer, a guide, a signpost. Reading alone cannot be the completion of the journey. It is only the first step; read for the sake of practicing, not for reading's sake. Too many books in a room indicate a person suffering from intellectual illness, just as too many tins, capsules and bottles of medicines in a cupboard indicate that the person is suffering from physical illness.

When calamity approaches, discrimination departs.

    You cannot destroy anger by anger, cruelty by cruelty, hatred by hatred. Anger can be subdued only by forbearance, cruelty can be overcome only by non-violence, hatred yields only to charity and compassion.

Politics without principles,
Education without character,
Science without humanity, and
Commerce without morality
Are not only useless, but positively
Dangerous.

Human virtues cannot be acquired from others. They cannot be nourished by the mere study of books. Nor can they be got ready-made from teachers. They have to be cultivated by each person and the resulting joy has to be experienced by him.

Health and Wholeness

You must try to develop physical well-being and health, for a gem has to be treasured in a safe, strong box. The gem of Divinity that is your reality also has to be kept in a strong box, namely, the body.

Drop the delusion that you have become old or diseased, or that you have become weak and debilitated. Some people begin to count the years and grieve over advancing age and shudder like cowards afraid of Death. But remember, **elation is Heaven, despondency is hell.** Have always some work to do and do it well that you get joy.

Joy derived through service reacts on the body and frees you of disease.

Namasmarana [continual remembrance of and contemplation on the name of God] is the best means. Only you do not really believe that it can cure or save you: that is the tragedy. People believe in the efficacy of only costly, brightly packaged, widely published drugs; the simple easily available remedy which is in everybody's backyard is ignored as useless.

The secret of perfect health lies in keeping the mind always cheerful! Never worried, never hurried, never borne down by any fear, thought or anxiety.

Illnesses are caused not so much by the food people eat or the conditions in which they live, but by mental weakness and mental attitudes, prejudices and predilections. Desires, disappointment, despair – they also cause diseases.

Anger is another enemy of health. It injects poison into the bloodstream.

Fear is the biggest cause of illness.

Too much food results in dullness of mind.

By eating flesh one develops violent tendencies and animal diseases.

Drink milk, or yogurt, eat fruits and nuts. They generate constructive, virtuous, spiritual thoughts.

Treat the distressed, the diseased, the old, the help-less, the child, with great respect and intelligent consideration.

The Present

Remember that the present is the true friend; yesterday has deceived you and gone; tomorrow is a doubtful visitor. Only today is the surest, best friend; hold fast onto it.

Truth

How can man realize the Truth? Only when he experiences non-dualism. As long as he is steeped in dualism (that he and the Divine are different), he is bound to be racked by the opposites: joy and sorrow, the real and the unreal.

God Realization

No one can conceive of the Almighty without picturing It as Power, Light, Mercy, Wisdom, Energy, Intelligence, Purity.

God has four qualities and it is only when you cultivate them that you can understand Him. They are: *Prema* (Love), Beauty (*Soundarya*), Sweetness (*Madurya*) and Splendor (*Shoba*). The development of *Prema* is enough to add into you the other three. When you are full of *Prema* for the Divine in all creation, that stage is Beauty; when you are immersed in the sea of Universal Love, you reach the acme of Sweetness; when your mind loses its identity and merges in the Universal Mind, then there is Splendor indescribable.

If we safeguard Righteousness, it will, in its turn, safeguard us.

God Immanent

Placing God at a great distance and praising Him as omniscient, omnipotent, omnipresent will not please Him. Develop nearness, proximity, kinship with God.

God is not to be spoken of as coming down or going up, since He is everywhere.

Expansion

Expand yourselves; do not contract into your own tiny individuality.

Expansion is my life. When you expand individual life to infinity it becomes divinity.

An Attitude for All Times ℭ℞

Thomas Alva Edison was possibly the greatest inventor ever. Once, asked to sign a hotel guest book that queried what he was interested in, he wrote, "Everything."

DCJ (Fadiman, Anecdotes, 182-83)

Surrender

The word "surrender" in English is not quite correct, it is not the right word .... Because, when you say "surrender" you are separate and God is separate. That is the meaning you get. But God is not separate.

It is not a question of surrendering or giving to some other one. One surrenders to himself. Recognition that the *Atma* is oneself is surrender. Surrender really means the realization that all is God, that there is nobody who surrenders, that there is nothing to be surrendered, nor is there anyone to accept a surrender. All is God. There is only God.

Hislop: "Surrender" is not really a very good word. It quite fails to convey what is meant.

"Surrender" is world language. To correctly describe [it], language of the divine is needed. There is no adequate word in the English language, therefore the use of "surrender" goes on.

You must have not only freedom from fear, but freedom from hope and expectation. Trust in my wisdom; I do not make mistakes. Love my uncertainty! For it is not a mistake. It is my intent and will. Remember, nothing happens without my will. Be still. Do not want to understand; do not ask to understand. Relinquish understanding. Relinquish the imperative that demands understanding.

Meditate upon the feeling between waking and sleeping, knowing how immediate, how close, how deeply compatible it is. There is the feeling of really giving up: the body is limp. Awareness too is limp. Let the feeling of God overcome you like sleep.

Do all acts as offerings to God; do not classify some as "my work" and some as "His work."

The highest virtue is humility, surrender to God.

Deleting and Desisting

❧

Deleting Anger

One attack of anger exhausts three months of health. Man should conquer anger by means of fortitude and conquer hatred by means of love. Do not feed anger with retaliation and do not feed hatred with fury.

Anger is the harvest of the bewitching mind; it enslaves man and fogs his understanding.

Anger is the worst exhibition of the ego.

Deleting Attachment

"Monkey-minds," Baba – what do you mean?

It is a kind of mentality that is used by the peasants to trap and destroy monkeys. When the peasant wants to catch a monkey, he uses a big pot with a narrow mouth as a trap. Inside the pot he puts edibles which the monkey loves. The monkey finds the pot and puts its paws inside it to grasp as much of the stuff as he can hold. Once it does so, it is unable to pull its paws out from the small mouth of the pot. It imagines that someone inside the pot is holding its paws, so it struggles and attempts to run away with the pot, only to fail and get trapped. No one is holding the monkey; it has trapped itself because of its greed. If only it lets the stuff in its paws go, it will be free of the bondage.

In the same way, I tell the rich people, man is tempted by the wealth, pleasures and desires of the world. When he gets lost in such attachment and suffers the consequences of greed, he thinks that something is binding him down, capturing him, destroying him. He does not realize that he himself is responsible for this bondage. The moment he gives up material wealth and desires, he will be free.

No one can liberate you, for no one has bound you. You hold on to the nettle of worldly pleasure and you weep, like the kite is pursued by the crows so long as it carries the fish in its beak; once the kite drops the fish, immediately it is free. So you too should give up attachment to the senses; then sorrow and anxiety can harass you no more, and you will be happy.

When a cat kills your pet parrot, you are enraged; when it kills a mouse, you are pleased. Though the behavior of the cat is the same, you desired one and disliked the other, as a result of your attachment! Desires are decided by personal prejudice and fancies.

Do not get attached to worldly things and pursuits. Be in the world, but do not let the world be in you.

Deleting Attack

If you destroy or disturb the faith of others or the devotion of others, it is ingratitude, treason; it is like pouring glowing cinders on a heap of flowers.

Do not use poisonous words against anyone, for words wound more fatally than even arrows.

Do not entertain bad feelings about anyone. They do you more harm than to others.

Do not seek to discover or discuss the evil in others, for the attempt will tarnish your own minds!

Do not blame others by pointing out their faults. You will find, upon self-examination the faults you see in others are in you. When you correct yourself, the world becomes correct.

Deleting Desires

Who is the poorest man in the world?

Hislop: The man without God?

No. The man with the most desires is the most poor. Until we realize the desireless state of pure bliss, we are in poverty.

Desire for worldly objects produces pleasure and pain, whereas desire for God confers bliss and does not produce pain.

The happiness in life will be in inverse proportion to your desires. In the journey of life, as in a railway journey, the less luggage (desires) you carry, the greater the comfort.

Deleting Doubt

Doubting . . . clips the wings of joy; it dampens enthu-
siasm, it tarnishes hope.

Deleting Ego

Egoism makes man see glory in petty achievement,
happiness in trivial acquisitions, joy in temporary authority
over others.

Criticizing others, finding fault with them – all this
comes out of egoism.

Jealousy and anger are the twins born of egoism.

Ego, the Fraud ❦

Samuel Goldwyn, the movie magnate, once had a ghostwriter draft several articles purportedly by Goldwyn. When the writer grew ill, a second penman was called. Reading a piece from the new man, Goldwyn grumbled, "That's not at all up to my usual standard."

DCJ (Fadiman, Anecdotes, 248)

The ego brings wave after wave of wants and wishes before your attention and tempts you to gain them. It is a never-ending circle.

Envy and greed also emanate from the ego and have to be carefully watched and controlled. Like a tadpole's tail the ego will fall away when you grow in wisdom. Ego must fall away; if it is cut the poor tadpole will die. So, don't worry about the ego; develop wisdom.

Hislop: Swami once said that the world emerges outward from man, just as human beings emerge outward from the body of the mother. Does this mean the entire world of which we are aware, everything?

There is one exception. There is one thing that comes into man from the outside. That thing is the ego which is formed by attachment to outside objects. With desire for the world cut, ego automatically vanishes.

The Comeuppance of the Emperor's Ego ❧

Following the disaster in Russia, Napoleon raced back to France with a bare escort, ahead of his defeated troops. Reaching the River Neman, he asked a ferryman whether many French deserters had come that way. "No," said the Russian, "you are the first."

DCJ (Fadiman, Anecdotes, 421)

Deleting Envy

The Truth can flash only in a mind clear of all blemishes. The first blemish that I would like to warn you against is: "inability to bear the success of others." Envy is the greatest of the sins. Vanity, envy and egoism are kin. They cut at the root of man's real nature.

Deleting Evil

When you feel you cannot do good, at least desist from doing evil.

Deleting Fixation on the Fruits of Action

If you have an eye on the fruits of your actions, you are liable to be affected by worry, anxiety, and restlessness.

Deleting Lack of Foresight ଓଃ

Teddy Roosevelt, Jr. was the son of President Theodore Roosevelt. Having arranged to meet his wife's train, he was at the station when the train swept by at full speed. Frantically, his wife waved from the rear car and tossed an envelope onto the tracks. As the car disappeared, Roosevelt recovered the message, which read — "Dear Ted: This train doesn't stop here."

DC J (Fadiman, Anecdotes, 477)

Deleting Bad habits

There are no mountain peaks to climb, just drop habits one by one.

My Grace is proportional to your effort. Try to win grace by reforming your habits, reducing your desires and refining your higher nature.

Suffering and misery are the inescapable acts of the cosmic drama. God does not decree these calamities but man invites them by way of retribution for his own evil deeds. This is corrective punishment which induces mankind to give up the wrong path and return to the right path so that he may experience the godlike condition of sat-chit-ananda – that is, an existence of wisdom and bliss. All this is part of the grand synthesis in which the negatives serve to glorify the positives. Thus death glorifies immorality, ignorance glorifies wisdom, misery glorifies bliss, night glorifies dawn.

Deleting Ignorance

Ignorant people seek joy and contentment from external objects, though there are treasures inside them. They arise from the Lord who is inherent in them, everywhere. Underground we have a stream of potable water; between us and the stream there is a thick bed of soil. By spiritual work that soil has to be removed. So too, peace and contentment exist deep within the consciousness of everyone, but they are overlaid by thick beds of evil tendencies and habits (greed, hatred, lust, desire, pride, jealousy, attachment to the outer world) and so, man has to remove these in order to benefit from the treasure.

Deleting Judgment

No one can judge another, for when another is judged you are yourself condemned.

Deleting Luggage

Reduce the luggage you carry about, when on the journey of life.... The mind, the senses, the intelligence, the imagination, the desires, the plans, the prejudices, the discontent, the distress – all are items of luggage. Jettison them soon to make your travel lighter, safer and more comfortable.

Deleting Mind

Your mind is the cause of your inability to understand the real nature of the world. The characteristic of the mind is Pravrithi – external orientation.

The mind is very subtle and expansive. It is light and pervasive, floating hither and thither on any gust of desire. It behaves like a ball of cotton, with no weight of seed to hold it down. It is much lighter than fluff; it wanders far and wide.... The mind is fickle and free. It flees as far as it fancies.

The mind can be compared to the Peepal tree. The Peepal leaves are always shaking whether there is a wind or not. Similarly, the mind is always unsteady and wavering. In addition to its wavering quality, the mind is also strong, and it can be quite cruel, too.

The mind is only another name for a bundle of desires, seeking and avoiding . . . . It is always given to ruminating over something. It is easy to affix the mind on something but it is very difficulty to withdraw it. The mind is at all times engaged in internal talk with itself and planning some scheme or the other. The talk goes on wandering in a wayward manner. The planning . . . centres around the solution for a continuous stream of problems that present themselves.

We must try to overcome this tendency of endless dialogue inside the mind.

Give the mind rest from constant involvement with ideas and solutions, or else it suffers pollution through dwelling on the faults and failings of others and through contemplation on external affairs. The mind, like a carbon paper, gets imprinted with the thoughts that pass through it, so spiritual progress is halted and the mind is contaminated with the evil on which it dwells. It gets distracted and disturbed.

There are three methods by which the mind can be silenced and steadied: (1) Pranayama: The regulation of the breathing process by inhaling and exhaling in measured sequence and with one-pointed attention. This will still the waves in the mind. (2) Social Service: When the mind is engaged in some service program, instructing people and teaching them holy thoughts and ideals, nursing and comforting the sick or some such selfless activity to help others who need it, this will stop the ceaseless talk it engages in. (3) Sadhana [spiritual practices]: Kirtan, Bhajan [both devotional songs], Yogasanas [Yoga exercises] and Japa [repetition of a mantra or name of God]. These can calm the mind and quiet the agitated conversation therein. The Gayatri mantra is very beneficial for this purpose of controlling or stilling the wandering mind.

The mind is like a boulder which the intellect transforms into an image, as a sculptor does. If the intellect allows the senses to dictate the design, the boulder will be shaped into a horrid idol. If, however, the senses are sublimated by the spirit, the image wrought by the intellect will be simply adorable. One must have the mind fully cooperating in the spiritual discipline and not obstructing its progress at every step. Liberation is the goal and the mind must help the pilgrim at every state of his journey. The mind should not admit any activity that is contrary to Dharma or injurious to spiritual progress.

The mind sees separateness, Love sees unity.

Hislop: Where do thoughts go?

They go no place.... The mind goes out and grasps and gets entangled in thoughts. If desire is for God, the mind does not go out. But the best way is not to have the problem of getting rid of thoughts. The best way is to see all thoughts as God. Then only God-thoughts will come.

One has, therefore, to rise beyond the mind to consciousness to achieve self-realization. To gain the infinite, universal *Atma*, the embodied self must break out of the puny, finite little prison of individuality.

Deleting Offense

When you do not accept the insult someone casts on you, it goes back to the person who indulged in it first; a registered letter that is not accepted returns to the sender. Do not damage your mental peace by receiving the letter and reading the contents. Refuse to receive it.

Deleting Past Consciousness

Let go of the past. Stop trying to get from each other what you still think you missed in childhood or in marriage. You will never find anyone who is enough – not even Me. Love Yourself, Know Yourself, Be Yourself. Only You will ever be enough.

The Sanyasi [ascetic] has to declare his death and perform obsequies for himself and bury his past. He destroys all that binds him to the rest and to his past, his history and his name. He avoids any reminder of his erstwhile adventure and the pursuit of sensory joy. He flees from his friends and foes, his habits, and habiliments, his hobbies and prejudices. But we find men who have taken the vow of Sanyas [abandoning attachments to worldliness] still clinging to their long established practices and habits. Instead they must completely break with the past.

Deleting Preaching before Acting

Do not scatter advice without the authority born of practical experience.

Act and then advise; practice first, precept second.

Deleting Prejudices

Ordinary people think that the joy or pain which they get from being with people whom they like or dislike, comes from those people; but it is not so. It is one's own likes and dislikes which are responsible for one's joy or sorrow.

Light spreads; it mingles with the light from other sources of light; it has no boundaries, no prejudices, no favorites.

Deleting Pride

Spiritual pride is the most poisonous of all varieties of pride; it blinds and leads the person suffering from it into ruin.

Man imagines that he has achieved much as a result of his search for material pleasures. He has discovered electricity and is using it for giving light. But what poor glory is this? When the sun rises even the brightest bulb pales into insignificance. Man has invented the fan, and, by means of electricity, he is able to create a breeze. But, when a storm arises in Nature, the toughest tree is uprooted and man's handiwork of brick and mortar is laid in ruins, with the roofs flying in the air. On what basis can he erect his pride?

Deleting Procrastination

If you decide that a particular activity is good and sacred, you should not postpone it.

Procrastination turns even ambrosia into poison.

Not Taking the Part for the Whole ○ᴚ

As a young man, the English poet, Alfred Lord Tennyson, suffered grievously from piles. Fortunately, relief came at the hands of a famous proctologist. Years later, after Tennyson had become poet of the realm, he was afflicted again, and sought out the same proctologist. Expecting to be recognized as famous himself now, he was at first disappointed — until he bent over, and the good doctor exclaimed, "Ah Tennyson!"

DCJ (Fadiman, Anecdotes, 537–38)

Deleting Self-Disparagement

The Divinity you have as the core of your being, you ignore; at the same time, you seek it in others. That is the tragedy. You insult yourself by feeling helpless, weak and inferior. Cowardice and self-condemnation, these do not become a spark of the Divine Flame.

Deleting Servility

Do not become a slave to others; no, not even to God.

Deleting the Notion of Sin

Sin is not the real nature of man. Sin is acquired and can be shed . . . . I have stopped people from reciting sayings that proclaim man to be sinful, born in sin. Do not condemn yourselves as weak, sinful, conceited, etc.; when doing that, you condemn Me, your Inner Self. I dislike people condemning themselves as sinners; it is treason to their Inner Reality. Self-condemnation is . . . egoism.

Deleting Love of Struggle and Suffering

Do not count your tears of pain; do not pour over your griefs. Let them pass through your mind, as birds fly through the sky, leaving no trail behind.

Deleting Negative Thoughts

If man wishes to be happy, the first exercise he must do is to remove from his mind every bad thought, feeling and habit.

Ideas of suicide, let "Me" tell you, are born out of the most despicable form of cowardice. Do not allow them to affect you; be bold, so bold that you are determined to brave out any calamity that you may assail. When you have God installed in your heart, who can lead you to destruction?

Deleting Violence

We generally think that AHIMSA (non-violence) means not causing harm to some living being. Ahimsa is not just this. Even bad thoughts or bad hearing or bad talk is HIMSA (violence).

The Feeling of
Enlightenment

જી

My dears: The time will come when the whole of this dream will vanish. To everyone of us there must come a time when the whole universe will be found to have been a mere dream, when we shall find that the soul is infinitely better than its surroundings. In this struggle through what we call environments, there will come a time when we shall find that these environments were almost zero in comparison with the power of the soul. It is only a question of time, and time is nothing in the infinite. It is a drop in the ocean. We can afford to wait and be calm.

As one turns to God with stronger love, the world recedes, appearing smaller until it can hardly be noticed at all.

The real nature of Avatars is that they are always overflowing with the spirit of delight and joy. Just as the ocean rises and surges up when there is a full moon in the sky, in the same way when I look at the devotees, My Heart overflows with limitless, boundless love for them.

Do you realize the ocean has limits? I have none.

Where there is faith, there is love;
Where there is love, there is peace;
Where there is peace, there is God;
And where there is God, there is bliss.

Measure the heights you have reached with the yard-stick of virtue, serenity, fortitude and equanimity.

A "Mahatma" is one in whom the thought, word and deed are harmonious and one.

Benefits ೫

Charles Steinmetz (d. 1923) was an American electrical engineer, a contributor to electrical theory and an important inventor. After his retirement, General Electric recalled him for advice on the breakdown of complex machinery that had stumped all experts. Strolling around the machinery, Steinmetz tested this and that, and then promptly chalk-marked an X on one engine. The GE men dismantled the engine and discovered the flaw at the exact spot.

A little later, General Electric received a bill for $10,000.

Shocked, the company demanded an itemizing of expenses.

Steinmetz wrote back —
Making one chalk mark ... $1

Knowing where to place it ... $9,999

DCJ (Fadiman, Anecdotes, 523)

Hislop: The mind has the tendency to plan ahead. No doubt this is a wrong activity?

In ordinary life, one makes plans and carries them out. This has to continue, with purity, and without harm to others. At length, a spontaneous divine thought will arise without planning. Such divine impulses will continue.

Hislop: Is it true that wild animals will not harm a saintly person?

There was once a guru who told his disciple that God was in everything. The disciple believed the statement. That very day there was a royal parade. The king was the centre of attraction riding on an enormous elephant. Ignoring the rules of safety for such parades, the disciple planted himself firmly in the path of the royal elephant, and he paid no attention to the cries of warning that he would be trampled to death. Upon reaching him, the elephant lifted him and put him safely to one side. The disciple went to the guru and complained that although God was in both the elephant and himself, he had been unable to remove the elephant from his path. That, on the contrary, the elephant had removed him. The guru explained that it was merely a matter of the elephant having greater physical strength. He told the disciple that had he not been looking at God in the elephant the beast would have killed him just as a matter of ordinary work. However, since the disciple was looking at God in the elephant, God had safely lifted him out of harm's way. No animal, not even a cobra, will harm the person who sees God as the essential reality of the animal or the snake. The same is usually true as regards dangerous men, but there are some exceptions there because of karmic implications.

What science has been able to unravel is merely a fraction of the cosmic phenomena; it tends, however, to exaggerate its contribution.

Science is a mere glow-worm in the light and splendor of the sun. It is true that it can research, discover and gather a lot of information about nature and its material functions and use it for the development of worldly things. Spiritualism, on the other hand, reigns over the cosmic field where science has no place. That is why some discoveries of science are useful while others can be disastrous.

Science is a way of looking at the outer world through the mind. The mind's nature is duality; it divides reality into different names and forms – it dissects, compares, contrasts, separates, categorizes – tries to define and bind reality in terms of words and concepts.

All of this cosmos – the entire material universe, as vast an expanse as it seems – is just a flake of froth, a bubble, on the ocean of reality. You are the ocean. You're not the flake of froth and you're not the wavelet – you are beyond separation. You are everything – you are the ocean.

The mind sees separateness, duality; but there is another way of experiencing reality – as unity. It is through the heart, by the process of love. Love reaches out to merge with the other; two become one. Loves sees unity. For the limited little wavelet self to know that it is the ocean, it must merge back into the ocean – through love.

The scientist says, "What is this" – this which lies in the outer world and is seen through the senses. The spiritual aspirant says, "What is that" – that which lies beyond the outer world and the senses, beyond duality and the mind as well. "That" is the ocean from which all "this" arises.

Why is it that everybody says "I"? She says "I," he says "I," you say "I"; we all look different but there is this common sense of "I"-ness. What is the meaning behind this? We have to look beyond this constantly changing world of different names and forms in order to see the underlying, unchanging and immutable reality: the reality that always was and always will be, the underlying unity which gives rise to all this diversity. How can the scientist with his mind try to grasp unity? The mind sees separateness; love sees unity. The only way that the wavelet can know the ocean is to merge back into it – to become one with it. Love is the way; merge with love, through your devotion to God.

My name is Sathya, truth. I represent that which is beyond mind. I have come to show you who you are – the reality that lies beyond the mind.

The moment you see your own beauty and are so filled with it that you forget all else, you are free from all bonds; you know that you are all beauty, all the glory, all the power, all the magnitude of the Universe.

After long searches here and there, in temples and in churches, in earths and in heavens, at last you come back. Completing the circle from where you started, to your own soul and find that He for whom you have been seeking all over the world, for whom you have been weeping and praying in churches and temples, on whom you were looking as the mystery of all mysteries shrouded in the clouds, is nearest of the near, is your own self. The reality of your life, body and soul. That is your own nature. Assert it, manifest it. It is truth and truth alone, that is one's real friend, relative.

Sathya Sai Baba

Sources ଓଃ

Hundreds of books in English alone exist by or about Sathya Sai Baba. Three wide-ranging books of his quotations, Murty's *Digest* and *Digest 2* and Sahni and McClung's *Gems of Wisdom*, cover together 1200 pages. At last count, there were at least fourteen volumes of Baba's commentaries in *Summer Showers in Brindavan*, twenty-one volumes of his *Vahini* (stream) series, and thirty-nine volumes of *Sathya Sai Speaks*. There are also numberless insights given by Baba to individual devotees.

Select Bibliography:

Drucker, Al. *Sai Baba Gita, The Way to Self-Realization and Liberation in this Age.* Crestone, CO: *Atma* Press, 1998.

Fadiman, Clifton, ed. *The Little, Brown Book of Anecdotes.* Boston: Little Brown, 1985.

Haraldsson, Erlendur. *Modern Miracles: An Investigative Report on Pyschic Phenomena Associated with Sathya Sai Baba.* Mamaroneck, NY: Hastings House, 1997.

Hislop, John S. *Conversations with Bhagavan Sri Sathya Sai Baba.* Prasanthi Nilayam, India: Sri Sathya Sai Books & Publications Trust, n.d.

———. *My Baba and I.* Prasanthi Nilayam, India: Sri Sathya Sai Books & Publications Trust, n.d.

Hawley, Jack. *Reawakening the Spirit in Work: The Power of Dharmic Management.* San Francisco: Berrett-Koehler Publishers, 1993.

Kasturi, N. *Sathyam Sivam Sundaram.* 4 vols. Prasanthi Nilayam, India: Sri Sathya Sai Books & Publications Trust, n.d.

Krystal, Phyllis. *Sai Baba: The Ultimate Experience.* Longmead, England: Element Books, 1990.

———. *Taming Our Monkey Mind: Insight, Detachment, Identity.* York Beach, ME: Samuel Weiser, 1994.

Mason, Peggy and Ron Laing. *Sai Baba: The Embodiment of Love.* Bath, England: Gateway Books, 1993.

McMartin, Grace J. *Seva – A Flower at His Feet.* Prasanthi Nilayam, India: Sri Sathya Sai Books & Publications Trust, n.d.

Murphet, Howard. *Sai Baba: Man of Miracles.* York Beach, ME: Samuel Weiser, 1971.

———. *Sai Baba: Avatar.* San Diego: Birthday Publishing, 1977.

Murty, Tumuluru Krishna. *Digest: Collection of Sri Sathya Sai Baba's Sayings.* Milan: Sathya Sai Foundation, 1985.

———. *Digest 2: Collection of Sri Sathya Sai Baba's Sayings.* Hyderabad, India: Dr. T. Gowri Tumuluru & Co., 1994.

———. *Sai Avatar.* Vol. 11. Calcutta: C. J. Gandhi Welfare Trust, n.d.

Sahni C. M. and Robert McClung. *Gems of Wisdom: Quotations from Bhagawan Sri Sathya Sai Baba.* Puttaparthi, India: Sri Sathya Sai Books & Publications Trust, n.d.

Sandweiss, Samuel H. *Sai Baba: The Holy Man . . . and the Psychiatrist . . .* San Diego: Birthday Publishing, 1975.

———. *Spirit and the Mind.* San Diego: Birthday Publishing, 1985.

Sathya Sai Baba. *Sathya Sai Speaks: Discourses of Bhagavan Sri Sathya Sai Baba.* Vol. 18. Prasanthi Nilayam: Sri Sathya Sai Books & Publications Trust, 1986(?).

Thomas, Joy. *Life is a Dream: Realize It!* Beaumont, CA: Ontic Book Publishers, 1992.

Webpages:

Sathya Sai Baba website:
http://sathyasaibaba.net/

International Sai Organization:
www.sathyasai.org

Sathya Sai Baba Book Center of America
www.sathyasaibooks.com

Sri Sathya Sai Book and Information Centre,
290 Merton Street,
Toronto, ON M4S 1A9
www.saibooks.org

❧ Notes ☙